You Who Took the Boat Out

By

Alison Hicks

Published by Unsolicited Press
Copyright © 2017 Alison Hicks
Cover Design: Savannah Stewart
All Rights Reserved.
ISBN-13: 978-0998087214

For Charlie and Jeremy, fellow paddlers

Table of Contents

I. Whirlpool

Centrifuge

In college he took me up to see it.
I peered inside the shiny disc; it gave no clue.

No ceremony but notice to vacate.
The lab transported nine years ago
in a moving van whose freezer gave out en route.
How do you give up a life?

Seventeen years. If I burn a pinch of sage, strike the bowl,
what rises?

At the pond

he rested a foot on the split-rail fence.
I kept looking at his Nike.
I didn't want to hear.
I was always sneaking looks at his body,
the long and graceful hands, turning out now,
in emphasis, the jeaned, bended knee.
My feet in sandals wet with dew.

This couldn't have taken nearly as long
as I am making out. I must have been forming
a reply, more than that, something to keep him,
and could I have known then in some way,
did I feel the drawing down of the comb
the parting to lift and braid?
The twist, and then the next.

The Hike

As we wound around boulders,
I tried to answer, explain
my two-chambered heart.

By the time we reached
the meadow and the wildflowers,
I was a woman lying down in long grass.

The sun was out, the valley spread before us.
The ridge revealed itself
climbing out of the hollow.

The Forest She Knows

A length of wood is made to curve
gently bending adding water
bending wetting and bending
the shape remembered
when the grain relaxes

to be well-loved might feel like that

ink spreading onto paper
rain sliding down a pine needle
foot on a floorboard in summer
crescent of sweat pulled in
as the foot pulls free

Blue Ridge

Velvet soil, sliced like cake.
I stepped over the gate, the sign, *No Trespassing.*
Up the grade, a dog blocked my path.
Pricked-up ears. Red as earth.
We watched each other. I took a step.
He did not move. A warning, I thought,
turned back.

The next day, I followed the eroded gully,
climbed to a place scraped flat
of trees and brush, living things pushed to the side,
a pile of dead, uprooted stumps.
The dog did not appear.

I had come to see, and did,
looking out to a spine I knew:
green and blue, rising and falling, longing
for what is not, desire
I could travel up and down, never see

the end. In this
no different from those
who so rudely pulled skin from this land.

Who had sent the dog,
had he been there at all or had I conjured him,
who and what was he protecting?

Red Eye

There's a skirt I wanted you
to see me in, short and silk.
—*Inner thigh the texture of a hard-boiled egg*—
My diaphragm a bellows
that stokes my heart, that punk.
My remembering body
sings back to headphones.
The man across the aisle snores.

The airliner moves like silk,
our conversation:
threads going one way
laid over those going another.
The bolt unwinds.
We chase dawn, losing time.

He Told Me It Would Happen

The ending hung over everything we did,
exchanging presents as we liked to do,
books and nuts and chocolate, over everything we'd done,
backroads, gas station neon in the August night,
the restaurant with the singer, tips in the jar,
how I ate a cherry tomato,
books we talked about, chocolate and nuts,
sound of bullfrogs and cicadas, a canopy
over everything we were about to.
Fog rose from the river.
We drove past the point we couldn't see
then opened windows and blasted heat. The future
settled on both sides of the windshield.

The Way Things Are

Will it do, can it be enough,
not yet I furnish with a bed, blue walls,
a window I couldn't open without wrenching?

The catch in my side, was that what I wanted
when I hoisted the sash, after he left,
then stuck the block between it and the sill?

To let the night in, turn off
the machine that cooled the air and covered our noise.

My noise, he said it turned him on,
those sounds come out of me.

So did he, did he let me, or did we agree
to stuff the washcloth in my mouth?

Not yet the scrape against the frame.

Feeder

I want to be the blossom,
hummingbird in on whirring wings.

Chocolate was the sugar water you left.
A song we did not play.

To be loved
unrealistically, what I need.

Your silhouette: curled feet, lowered beak
drinking my nectar.

Trees and Plants Rely on Wind and Bees

She might put on a silk dress with no sleeves
walk through an unmowed field in bare feet
show up where he's obviously going
just to show she can

She might name his faults
in such a way they're in need of tending
he's a garden: the body that takes up space

She *will* touch do the wrong things
familiar as she is with his objections
there are things she will not say
though he won't believe it

She might think of his boyhood
remind herself she had a girl's life
before she met him.

II. In a Big Country

Canoeing at Night

Rocks and logs you can't possibly.
Wood
in your palm.
The way it sweeps.

Stars have plunged into water.
Blaze back up.
Bodies shedding drops.

Loon with his red eye.
Where hurt happens.
Tasks completed.

You who took the boat out
understand.

Waking in Pain in the Early A.M.

In winter the gong sounds in the dark.
The *zendo* holds the *sangha*,
the mountains hold the *zendo*.

Residents bring a bowl,
something creamy and white and sweet.
She bows and thanks them and they sit.

She was barely dressed when they arrived,
pulled on dark sweatpants, a shirt.
She takes a spoonful, offers the dish around.

Something like ice cream, warmer and fluffier.
She would return to her room,
but a robed line blocks her door.

She has no question,
separated from her proper clothes.
Mountainside raised by the fire

that burns below the crust
bubbles into the water and at times
drops from the sky igniting the landscape.

Bowl filled with fire, ash,
ice, fire.

Red-Headed Woodpecker

knocks. His head swings back,
flouncing like a flamenco dancer's skirt.
He aims at the trunk, beak into wood,
hysterical child, woman in grief.

I let him in.
Hammering through my thick skull,
sweeping the gap with his narrow tongue.
Excavating, calling me to root.

At the Acupuncturist's

She lifts my wrists. Feels along veins & nerves & tendons.
Six pulses, *qi*.

What can she tell? I want to ask. What is she feeling that I feel?

She asks for my tongue.
I stick it out, gargoyle giving the raspberry to demons.

Head trauma?

No. Then I remember, first grade, recess, a crowd,
my head against asphalt, then pressed into the fur of a teacher's
          coat.
I called out the name that came to me:
the boy in my class who got blamed for everything.

Bump on my forehead.
My mother said, you must tell them, you don't know it was him.
Too much trouble to change my testimony.

A wheel, wooden algaed slats, water pouring over.
Who can say why one thing sticks, another floats away?

About things that don't get spoken, the seductions
you perform in the dark before sleep?

Why have I not by now attained for myself some arcane wisdom?
Herbs, names of plants, identification of mushrooms, paths of meridians?

Polka dots across my back. Fingers press, depress flesh.
Needles glide in.

Three Short Poems
for Trudy and The Porches

i. Sounds of the Porches

Cicada buzz, hummingbird wings,
squeaks when you get close.
Drunken hover, tail feathers fan,
black and white.
A train grinds through.
At dusk, a single cow low.
Whip-poor-will.
Mist rises along the river.
And the moon, the moon.

ii. The Path Between the Porches and the Schoolhouse

Walking to Helen's,
sitting on the bench in the hollow.
Cicada sound. Damp.
I am alone in a big country,
what I hold within myself.

iii. From the Upper Porch

The river unseen
below the trees
beyond the road and railroad tracks.
It's down there, somewhere.
Whip-poor-will that sounds like a loon.
Blue heron perches on its bank.
Cicadas sing rings around it—
Can you find it?
Can you find it?

Woman in the Leaves

In summer she burned—
tips of crape myrtle
at the bottom of the garden
through morning mist.

The first cool nights
she sings the leaves loose,
that float onto her hair
lodge in corners of her mouth.

She lies,
hips settling into moss.
Leaves blow and gather
in the crevices of her body.

Woman in the leaves,
the drop-dead leaves.

Prolapse

He told me. I knew
or at least suspected:
the soft, round head,
my middle age crowning.

The child I will not push out
lurks in the canal,
will never walk,
I cannot outrun.

Leaven

Beautiful woman, she said,
under her breath, searching my face for a name.
Does it matter?

Curls fell around her face.
Stirring the bowl, moistening dry ingredients.
Yeast frothing by a dirty window.

Why should it matter?

I used to say I wanted to be beautiful
so I would understand how to make beauty.
I'm not sure that's true. Mostly I thought I wouldn't blame myself.

Of course, I was wrong.
Does it come down to vanity?
But to rise into kneaded shape without complaint …

I didn't take it as flattery.
There was smoothness,
then minute bubbles rose, pocking the surface.

Guardians

You were the one who first saw them.
Canoeing toward Redpine Bay,
feeling sorry for yourself, you told me later,
and trying to talk yourself out of it.
In the bow I was dull, opaque.

You pointed. We hushed, dug in deeply,
tacking downwind until they came into focus:
shaggy, leggier than dogs.

Picking along the bay's curve,
they traveled together, just above the waterline,
until blocked by a rock.

One turned into the woods.
The other jumped in and swam around, got out, shook,
continued along the shore to the portage,
where he waited, fixed on us, then melted into trees.

You plunged from the canoe, splashed onto shore.
I paddled in.

When I stood in the place he had stood,
I thought I saw those eyes staring through the bush,
then they were gone, and I wasn't sure.

No way to follow.
Prints in sand gave out on harder ground.
The only proof: the photo, which we had to blow up
to show anything more than black dots.

Had they always been on separate errands,
did the paths they took converge?

First Peoples called them Night Guardians.

Or were they simply wolves, and we travelers in their territory?
Maybe all we are to each other.

Until I Let It Pass

The bird flew ahead—
wings spread and lift,
fold as she lands
a branch ahead.
She takes off as I approach,
to the next, and the next.
Tail feathers like a card shark's hand,
each time something different revealed:
white belly, gray wing,
until screened by evergreen.

Shouts from an athletic field
beyond the tennis courts,
impossible to tell the game.
I approach the bench
where I sat and cried—
need now blown free,
I thought I could make out a woodpecker's faint hammer.
Like the bird one tree ahead
of the heavy-footed thing
that accompanied me.

On the Soul

Dark bud
Opening and folding.

Hurts. Always.

Droplets of rain
Form lighted pathways.

Dancers escaped from bed
Leave worn-out shoes.

III. Floating Animal

Narcissus

We walked along the bank and couldn't find them.
Voices float in through walls, singing that won't be silenced.
Trying to match up what happened to the feeling.

The painting is not a boat, but we pitch like one.
Sounding against its fellows, broken at the hinge.

Keys fall through the grate.
Pink worm on the sidewalk.
Crocus heads too early dance.

Halloween

In our yard my son scatters plastic bones
in a Have-a-Heart trap
marked "Beware."

An evil jester with a black and red foolscap,
mask whose eyes we had to widen,
rallies his troops with a skull on a stick,
half Shakespeare, half Disney.

Upstairs in my office:
a bag of cow bones and two deer skulls.
A skeleton in a mariachi hat
plays guitar on my desk.

Wishbones

Bowlegged fantasies within my little finger's grasp.
Stealthily I stroke the springbacked bone
filled with such potential.
When I stand them back to back
they look like gunslingers.
The only way they can get out of this
is to walk backward away from each other,
turn and shoot, making someone's day.
Or placed the other way, they could be
loving, leg across leg.

Tissue Hearts

They were playing chess and the hearts flew all around.
He wore charcoal gray. She wore white. Both had red shoes.
He was about two inches taller, but she wasn't short.
She held a bishop in her hand. She had only recently learned.
He was about to make a move. She smiled, placing her right hand
against her cheek. She didn't always remember the moves he'd
      taught her.
He didn't seem to mind, would just shake his head a little,
resetting. She didn't take that as anything snide.
He was a statistician. He was going to a conference in a couple of
      weeks.
He asked if she'd go with him. She paused, fingering the bishop.
How many pawns to sacrifice? Not that she cared, particularly,
      about winning.
Okay she said and the hearts fluttered down. She caught one.
It was made of tissue paper, a little crinkled. She smoothed it out.
Others came down. Who was doing that, she wondered,
sitting above, dropping heart confetti down on them?
It fluttered to the floor and onto the table like leaves.
She caught one in the air, and it was a leaf.
He was sitting there smiling, not contemplating his move.
They had been indoors, in his kitchen with the black and white
      tiles
and the pale green walls, the lamp hanging from a cord.
The walls were now gone. It was snowing.
Snow collected on the board, piling on the pieces.
Red from her shoes bleeding into the snow.
She could no longer see the black tiles on the floor
or the black squares on the board. He was smiling as if nothing was
      wrong.
She reached over to touch him. He fell backward, like a piece of
      cardboard.
He was a piece of cardboard. She started to shiver.
Her hair was covered with snow. She shook and what came down
      was ash.
There was a smell in the air. The sky was orange and pink.
She pulled at her hair. The gray was not from the ash, but its color.
Her dress was loose and long; she had shrunk within it.
Before this moment, she had managed to stay calm.
A voice, somewhere behind her, said *Do you play chess*

The Strange History of M. Bernal

I will eat meringues at the Sorbonne
and leave a trail of glistening crumbs
that will spell out, in elaborate but predictable ways,
the code of codes that M. Bernal
has been seeking for some fifty years.
"Quel délice" he will exclaim
as he kneels to lift a crumb
between his thumb and forefinger,
inhales the essence of egg white and spun sugar,
understanding sweetness at last.

The knowledge will crack
his heart; it will creak like the hinges
of a suitcase, his chest will bifurcate.
When the gendarmes come
the small black ants that live under the floorboards
will have carried away the evidence
and the codes will go back
to being unreadable mysteries,
the way that air added to egg white
creates peaks and crevasses
that when baked turn glossy
and break like chalk under the teeth.

In the morning the students will flood in.
The headline in *Le Monde* declares
"M. Bernal est mort," and nobody knows why
he has left a devoted wife,
and in place of children 700,000 manuscript pages
written in a hieroglyphic
no one can comprehend.

Meanwhile, M. Bernal's soul
wakes up in the Amazon,
where it is happy to learn
that it can fly through the air
trailing colors.

Darwin's Barnacles

Lord Stanhope called it fiddle-faddle,
and after a week of sorting species
I nearly agree.

Through jungles and deserts
I uncovered uncharted geologies.
Now I suffer boils and swellings, digestive humors,
my *Cirripedia* my adventure.

In forms various—one sex or two,
females with extra males
tucked into valves of their shells—
who knew?

Eight years of barnacles—
better men than I spurned the task,
no taxidermist nor respectable naturalist—
small agencies, accumulated effects.

The floating animal grows a shell, attaches.
The wave moves down, up, down.
The shell—the work—bears witness.

Late-Night Rain

I've closed my files,
turned off the computer.
Padded into the bedroom,
sat down on the bed.

I stretch my feet,
luxuriate in their freedom,
remove my shirt, fabric brushing my face,
reach to undo my bra.

Staccato pings
skitter across tin,
echoing in the drainpipe.

As if someone out there
is typing out an idea
as fast as it comes,
before it moves on.

Secret

I hide it in my shoe, walk around on it,
let it bruise my toe, poke into my arch.

When I start to limp, and draw in my breath,
 I store it in my mouth.

Through the night it rides
a sea of spit, extra tooth in my craw,

where I grind down its ridges,
lay enamel over cracks.

When it emerges, round and nacreous
on my tongue, present it to you.

Behind the green fence

with the yellow top
aluminum twang

> *I was going to say . . .*
> *What I was going . . .*

in the outfield, running
ball bleached into sky

> *Did you hit, did I?*

knew something was wrong
when he didn't pick up
came out in passing
facts without details

> *I couldn't ask you . . .*
> *You don't have to . . .*

pictured a labyrinth
walking forward
steps curling

> *We will come back*

come watch the game
pitcher's windup
foot against the rubber
throw's arc, batter's judgment

> *The ball flew into its subject*
> *Like it was the sun*
> *And I an outfielder*
> *Glove outstretched for what might come down*

Spool

Loose thread on a branch.
From a jacket or sweater?
He picks it up between thumb and forefinger.
Pulls and it keeps coming, gathering in his hand.

When her mind starts unraveling,
it's clear the thread is her.

The yellow spider with the tortoiseshell back
has injected her with venom, wound her in silk—
he must find the red filament or give her up.

He sifts through the fallen leaves for it.
To guide through the eye, sew her back together.
Where are the helpers, gods or ants
to give him tokens, magic powers?

A thread hangs from her mouth.
It slips through her lips. He yanks it away.
The harder he pulls, the more avidly she swallows.

The spider's web of red threads
stretches across the path.
Though free, he is bound with her.

Red on the forest floor, splotches.
A labyrinth. He follows the curve,
circles and circles. She in the middle,
running fate through her fingers.

The Mother as Persephone

Call *Mama* into the hole?
Tear at its grassy sides, and finally go home
to the life that began with that opening?
What's a daughter to do.

She can hear her in her head.
She can come back to that meadow.
It makes no difference.
The hole fills in.

A figure who looks like her mother
sits down to table, eats lustily
from her plate, no longer understanding
the distinction between *yours* and *mine*.

When a mother grows crooked, bent,
what can a daughter do,
with no power to trade,
no gift to rescind from the world?

In the meadow, wildflowers bloom.
She puts her ear to the ground,
her blood will not open it.
Hades spits on her youth, wants nothing of her offerings.

Her mother has eaten the pomegranate.
With each seed she forgets a little more.

Blown-Down Tree

On my way
I pass the tree.
Roots
torn off
ugly earth
jammed.
Face stuffed
with mud
mouth filled with silt.
I hear
Mother's brain.
She calls.
She wants to be raised
root down
branch up.

Mermaid

I didn't want to walk.
Hot air blew my body.
I swam with currents.
They carried me.

*

Hans Christian told a tale,
steps that cut like knives.
She walked but couldn't keep up,
while he dallied with the two-
legged girls. Altered,
no way to return.

*

I understand sighing when skin breaks.
Rush of blood an out-breath.
She might have preferred it.
Each step calling, *here, here,*
walking into that voice.

*

On manatees,
keloids fibrous thatching
marks encounters with propellers.
Silkies they say can be persuaded
by human voice to unzip seal coats.
Even so, they are distracted,
return eventually to the sea.

*

On my two legs, I go down to the kitchen.
My father's cooking fills the house.
I swim up to the counter.
Mixer, rice maker,
canisters of sugar and flour.
I will make a cookie for my brother to eat.

*

I think I will never marry.
To whom could I tell
the swell of this house,
that lifts and plunges?
My father sighs in the night.
My mother's voice hidden
in the cushions of the sofa.

*

She grew a tail and swam
out the window.
I would like to join her
but will stay in this boat,
my sea-legs.

The Daughter Girds for Battle

You who would enter, stop.
In this house, do not.
I know what.
Not yours.
No desire?
Tell me again.
I do not believe.
Together they made us.
For him, only she.
If I let,
he will forget.

Queen of Night

I am a jewel in her gown,
set with the other motherless girls.
She asks for blood.
We comply.

We travel with her,
her cello soothes.
Black hair swaying, face in clouds,
she slips the moon into her pocket.

I am a paper doll.
She holds me up.
I gave what she asked.
They found me, brought me here.

Every day they ask if I hear. I do.
Abandoned, we are attuned.
Geodes on dusty museum shelves,
the only frequency that can crack us is hers.

She Stood on the Bank, the Ferry Did Not Come

Since her mother was sick
her father was the one who took her
to pick out a prom dress.

A strapless sheath,
blue as the Great Lakes,
left exposed the scars on her arms

that reproach him every time he looks,
even as they fade,
her body drawing them back inside.

You found her?
A long time before I felt I could ask.
The scene I'd imagined.

No, she came to me to say goodbye.
We were sitting in his car. We'd had lunch.
It was time to go, he had somewhere to be.

That means she wanted to live, I said.
No, he said. *She wanted to die.*

Origami

Only cranes, she says.
Fingers section the glossy square
by feel, turn the crease.

Sharp corners bend back.
Mind's wild thoughts
folded into each animal.

Pinned to a string with a bead,
red and gold and green,
they wait in the basket on her desk.

For the time she will raise her arms
and they fly up,
rising, circling.

Tornado of cranes,
flapping and calling,
only cranes.

Medium

A wooden canoe with varnished ribs, for instance.
Kevlar or epoxy can also be beautiful,
the lack of weight on shoulders.

It is good to make a craft that will carry
over lakes and rivers.

I should have worked with wood.
Just that the guys in shop class seemed so dull.

I know a man whose father was a millman.
He'd come home smelling of whatever wood
he'd worked that day.

My friend and his brothers and sisters learned
the smell of cherry, walnut, pine, oak.

I could carve a spoon so the grain
would show across the hollow.

I could make a table for you to sit down to,
that we could converse across.

Too bad the canoe factory in Peterborough
closed in 1961.

There would be no question of what I meant,
no misinterpretation, embarrassment.

A spoon, or a canoe.

V. Bioluminescence

Ventana

My husband and I were lost in the woods.
I want to hike from Esalen to Tassajara.
My dog has a notch in his ear.

Five days, four nights, twenty years ago.
Hot springs at either end.
He's a rescue, so we're not sure how he got it.

In the smallest wilderness area we've ever hiked.
Keep staring at maps.
Whether it caught on something and tore.

We couldn't have been more than a mile from our camp.
I want to empty myself into the landscape.
Or was deliberately done.

But we couldn't figure out how to get to it.
Feel fatigue behind my knees.
My husband thinks it was some kind of branding or marking.

We were tramping along a stream that dissipated into marshy
            ground.
Ridges plunging to the ocean.
He's calm most of the time, doesn't jump up, doesn't bark.

We were in a place we didn't remember.
Ocean that snatches the land.
Comes up to you, stands there and sniffs.

At night we took turns watching the fire.
Chaparral, grassy meadows, stands of pine.
Sometimes he'll startle and start to tremble.

When it was my turn to stay awake, I kept falling asleep.
Canyons of the Big Sur.
For no reason we can apprehend.

My turn to sleep, I couldn't.
Water rushing on.
Something we can't hear or smell.

I dreamed not of food but clean sheets.
Redwoods.
Maybe a memory.

Of Returning
For my parents

I live inside their deaths
a shaft of October light
through leaf litter
triangle of blue

the cup into which I put everything
what I knew about them
and I didn't what I didn't think to ask
what we held in common

our life of three sides
I could turn it over and it would never empty
it reaches through the stream
I do not know its contents

though I swim inside it and
press its sides it contains my birth and death
clear cloudy
above the dam

Autumn Lilies

In grief he'd call my mother's name.
My husband said, *I wish he wouldn't do that*—
Let him, I said.

                              The day he died
the sun was a flower at its peak.
I walked on the beach—
tide low, dipping my ankles
in warmed, orphaned pools.
Then placing my soles
on the wooden stairs
over the dunes
drifting back through quiet streets.

                              His lungs were full;
the hospice nurse turned over his hands.
Blue under his fingernails.
We waded in that pool with him
until it was over.

On my mother's birthday
I'd send him flowers.
Tulips, daisies, delphinium.
This year, lilies I ordered for myself
arrived in bud.

                              Three days in cool water.
I watched the waxy petals separate, curl back,
burst orange, yellow, red
pollen thick on the stamen,
dark specks near the base.

Cleaning the Skylights

My father through the skylight
in a cornflower work shirt
moving the sponge in circles
frowning in concentration
khaki work pants bucket of suds
brown water trickling down

roof not so high and mostly flat
hazard still for a 90-year-old man
never so angry as when his friend Tim
took the old wooden ladder away
cursed him out and went inside

California oaks rain debris
collects in corners
pebbles dropped by Steller's Jays
ping against the glass
he looked up once
to see a family of raccoons
parade across the top

the oak outside the kitchen
there when his parents bought the house
took out the neighbors' fence
in winter he went into the hospital
wood cut and stacked

through the glass pyramid
the moon's a smear
surf slams the beach

new staircase down the dunes
bright unweathered
a threatened species of lizard
burrows beneath ground cover
winter tides leave mounds of stinking kelp
uprooted from deep-sea anchors
my son and I can't resist stomping on the floats
he asks me to carry what he has collected
tells me the shape of the red Japanese gate

we pass on the way back means *water*

The Hospital, The Ship

From his locker we bring out
his copy of *Walden.*
The words are code.

By then he understands,
it isn't what he carries
as what's in him.

I was scared, he says and grips my arm.

The test, to call a sequence of colors.
If he didn't get them right,
casualties on all sides.

He strung a light,
read the works of Joseph Conrad,

to stay sane,
he told a friend years later:
I never thought the fucking war would end.

February Landscape

What's brewing below
How far do you have to go to be warm

Descend to some rage
That furnace that ticks on

Burns until the fuel's spent
Brine truck a porcupine

Creeping along arteries
Spraying white

Clichés of the season
Snowfields from the farmhouse

Sky in flannel
When I lived in a place without winter

Some complained of sunshine
Many wished aloud for rain

The monsoon in August
Slicked down burning streets

The desert hum
Rose from under ground

The House Two Doors Down

Old Mrs. Morrone, when she was dying,
would emit a noise
we'd hear when we walked by.

In register sometimes lower, sometimes higher,
constant, a sound not even animal,
a shriek from the side

she hadn't passed over to yet.
When I took my toddler son for a walk,
he would be afraid.

The sound lifting the air around him
existential—there and implacable,
protest.

I would hold his hand,
tell him it would be all right.
Mumble *look, we're almost home* before he could ask.

Honestly, I never knew her or her illness.
I did not ask my neighbors, who did,
What's the deal with Mrs. Morrone and that sound?

It was something not to talk about,
to respect and walk the long way around.
I was afraid they'd say, *What sound?*

Hardy

Growing up in granite and winter

I should be

He was hardy

Missed the seasons

Vermont streams

Water so cold

For a while he'd bathe every day

Wade into the Pacific

After my mother died

A friend wrote

It looked like he wanted to keep walking

"Into that beauty Jeffers loved"

Illumination

Late afternoon red-honey drips.

Three long strands in the hairbrush.
Unwound:

gold and red and brown.

Green Line

My son drinks lavender soda,
holds out a chocolate croissant
with the chocolate scooped out.

Outside, a man dances in the street.
Inside, a man reads.

The crackhead taps on the glass.

It's the anniversary of my father's death.
In an Italian folk tale, death is trapped in the tree,
scarfing down cherries, juice running down his chin.

Four men, now three, I love above others.
I look around, think I could love every man here.

Death in the tree, can't get enough of those cherries.

A woman greets me by name. I have no idea who she is.
She's older than when I last saw her.
Mara, she says.

A Mara interviewed me once. *Illusion*.
I liked her but she didn't hire me.

I pour myself a glass of champagne,
bottle heavy in my hand.

What we have to live with.
Death in the tree.

My husband and son play poker.
Nickel ante. Raise or call.

Prayers

whatever floats   opens   whatever gleams   dull

moves   whatever's still   calls   whatever's silent

whatever pangs   bounds   whatever takes   offers

laughs   whatever cries   travels   whatever turns

whatever wakens   sleeps   hurts   soothes

whatever waits   doesn't mind   not knowing   whatever rain

whatever dryness   cold   whatever warmth   ices

thaws

Variations

In Carmel in the fog,
in the house my grandfather bought and died before seeing,
the house my grandmother moved west for,
with the redwood in front, where she died,
and my father years later, on a sunny day at three in the afternoon.

Sandy hillside sliding toward the ocean.
Its sound rolling up streets.

Fog, because it's just not possible
for two people from the same family to die in sunshine in Carmel,
Jeffers' town, where I was born, at a hospital that no longer exists,
any more than one can die from migraine,
morning sun glassy by noon, cataracted.

Canoe

Pinching at the ends, widening in the middle
Floating silently except for the spiral
Behind now dying in the water

Tight bends must be approached
Steering toward the bank the river cuts into
Pivoting at the last minute

Seams must be fortified with pitch or epoxy
Remnants of a beaver dam make a dull creak across the bottom
Sometimes it will get stuck and you will have to step into the muck

Loading on land then picking it up at the ends will cause it to buckle
Large waves hitting the sides capsize it
Upside down, it still floats

Must be carried from one watershed to another
This involves uphills and downhills
Requires balance as well as strength

Hint of water through trees
Raises the heart to see
It feels good to lift the burden from shoulders

Cedar Lake

I'd seen them here before, the fall
we canoed past the male moose
standing in the shallows with their racks
and the sounds of the rut carried through the nights.

I had laryngitis but could imitate
the female's nasal vibrating bray.
I woke to cough, stumbling out to pee, unmistakable:
green streamers shooting up, pulsing waves.

Coughed a whole body hack.
By the time I'd finished it was fading.
The next morning my voice was back.

That was years ago, before the child,
asleep in his bag on an August night.
Slow-shifting white along the horizon:
northern lights.

Flying Thing

with feathers, beak and talon,
roman candle winging it toward clouds.

Is it true everybody's is the same?

So much harder to describe than brother melancholy.
To my dog, a molecule flying through his nose.

Walking at dusk, lights soft against leaves.

There might be a stream,
sometimes full and sometimes dry.

The whole damn thing flies off before you can identify it.

We were arguing, going back and forth,
should we hope for joy, can modest pleasure be enough?

The argument a pleasure in itself,
like the stream, the air, or the rocks.

Of course, they aren't mutually exclusive.

You know what I was saying:
there will always be those who, wisely or unwisely,
push beyond enough.

What I wish for you is what you want,
not what you might think you deserve,
nor what is realistic, nor possible.

The Soul Floats at the End of its Shell

i.
I held my father's hand as he died.
The hospice nurse traced the blue under his nails
described in the pamphlet
with the ship sailing off the cover.

Seawater rushes in one ear, out the other.

Two days later a dog came up
to me and my friend on the beach.
His nose brushed my leg.
Tall enough to pet without bending.
Still I continued talking
pulling the thread of some story I'd started.

He didn't seem to belong to anyone.
No one called him.
He stood panting, then took off into the spray.

ii.
Motor catching, turning over.
Not what you think but what happens when you let go of thinking.

iii.
If I had not wandered, could I be comforted,
had I not ventured into the rain
then asked to come in?

To coax myself into sleep
I've imagined love I've gathered
as heat in the center of my body.

Waking, stepped as if from a perfumed bath
fogging mirrors.

iv.
If the ball could be a body
soul what the pitcher lays on it
fingers splayed across the seam.

Wherever you look, it's somewhere else.

Our design unfolds,
bolt of cloth we weave and unweave.

Sometimes to remove the flaw,
sometimes to incorporate it.

Second Movement, Mozart Symphony #40

apple tree gone

  three-one-two

consumed from the inside out

  three-one-two-three

we brought it down last fall

  melting into the next phrase

before the wind

  notes open as flowers

now that corner of the yard lies open

  spring into summer

the apples were smaller each year

  I could talk about composition

until they disappeared

  tonic and dominant

round petals blow across the lawn

  the pulse descends

from a certain angle

  into my body

look like seeds or hail

  I could talk about tempo

an apple tree and a fireplace

    orchestration

scent gathering

    inside the phrase looking out

at the top of the stairs

    laps of sound lie down on top of each other
    and peel off

Notes

"He Told Me It Would Happen"—Cherry tomatoes, as well as the full-size version, also known as "pommes d'amour" in French, have traditionally been considered aphrodisiacs, it is speculated due to their color and shape.

"Waking in Pain in the Early A.M." —In Zen Buddhism, the *Zendo,*"meditation hall," is where *zazen*, sitting meditation, is practiced. A full-sized Zen temple will have at least one *Zendo*, however any place where people go to practice Zen can be referred to as a *Zendo. Sangha,* translated "association," "assembly," "company" or "community," traditionally refers to the monastic community of Buddhist monks and nuns, but can also be used more loosely to include lay practitioners.

"On the Soul"—The final stanza references Grimm's fairy tale "The Twelve Dancing Princesses," in which twelve princesses are locked up at night, yet their shoes are found worn out in the morning, as if they've been dancing all night, which, it turns out, they have been. The man who discovers their secret reveals it to the king, and gets his choice of the daughters as a bride.

"Halloween"—Figures of skeletons engaged in various human activities have become a prominent part of the holiday *Dia de Muertos*, the Day of the Dead, celebrated throughout Mexico, focusing on gatherings of family and friends to pray for and remember friends and family members who have died, and help support their spiritual journey.

"The Daughter as Mermaid"—This poem draws on three mermaid-related references. In Hans Christian Anderson's "The Little Mermaid," the mermaid, who has fallen in love with a human sailor, and desires a human soul so she can gain immortality, obtains from a Sea Witch a potion that will give her legs in return for tongue and her beautiful voice. The potion makes every step she takes feel like knives cutting into her body, and she can never return to the water. Manatees are possibly an early inspiration for the idea of mermaids. Silkies, also spelled selkies, are mythological creatures found in Scottish, Irish, and Faroese folklore, said to live as seals in the sea, but to shed their skins to become human on land. Though they may live as human for periods of time, they always desire to return to the sea.

"Prayers"—This poem is intended to be read two times, once left-right and then down-up, in either order.

"Variations"—This poem is informed by two widely-known poems, César Vallejo's "Black Stone Lying on a White Stone," with the first line, "I will die in Paris, on a rainy day," and Donald Justice's "Variations on a Text by Vallejo," with the first line "I will die in Miami in the sun."

"Flying Thing"—The first line plays on Emily Dickinson's "Hope is the Thing with Feathers.

Acknowledgements

The author cannot begin to express her gratitude to Leonard Gontarek and the Saturday Osage Poets, who helped incubate many of these poems; to Joan Houlihan, Martha Rhodes, and fellow participants in the Colrain Poetry Manuscript Intensive in January 2014, who offered stimulating comments on an early draft; to Trudy Hale and the Porches Writing Retreat, where successive drafts were put together; to Catherine Bancroft, Amy Small-McKinney, Chloé Miller, Therése Halscheid, and Hila Ratzabi for their poetic instincts, advice, and companionship; to Jane Hirshfield for her shining example; and to Rubie Grayson and Susan Stewart of Unsolicited Press, who saw merit in the manuscript and lent their talents to bring it to fruition.

She would also like to thank the publication in which the following poems first appeared, sometimes in slightly different form:
Apiary, "Mermaid," under the title "The Daughter as Mermaid"
Blood Lotus, "Tissue Hearts"
The Broadkill Review, "Prayers," "The Way Things Are"
Caliban Online, "Red-Headed Woodpecker"
Cottonwood, "February Landscape"
The Critical Pass Review, "Second Movement, Mozart Symphony #40"
Edison Literary Review, "At the pond"
EDGE, "Trees & Plants Rely on Wind & Bees"
Folly, "Darwin's Song of Barnacles"
Forge, "Spool"
Grey Sparrow, "The Blown-Down Tree," under the title "The Daughter and the Blown-Down Tree"
The Griffin, "Late-Night Rain"
Licking River Review, "Variations"
The Lindenwood Review, "Ventana"
The Louisville Review, "The Hospital, The Ship"
The Musehouse Journal, "Cedar Lake," "Until I Let It Pass,"
Organs of Vision & Speech, "The House Two Doors Down"
Passager, "She Stood on the Bank, the Ferry Did Not Come"
Permafrost, "Centrifuge," "Wishbones," "Woman in the Leaves"
Philadelphia City Paper, "Canoeing At Night"
Poetry Ink 14th Annual (Philadelphia, PA: Moonstone Arts Center, 2010), "At the Acupuncturist's"
Poetry Ink 15th Annual (Philadelphia, PA: Moonstone Arts Center, 2011), "Halloween," under the title "Bones"
Poetry Ink 20th Annual (Philadelphia, PA: Moonstone Arts Center 2016), "Flying Thing"

The Puritan, "The Soul Floats at the End of Its Shell"
Rio Grande Review, "Canoe"
Rougarou, "Narcissus"
Sanskrit, "Red Eye"
Studio One, "Medium"
Storyscape, "The Mother as Persephone," "Origami," under the title "The Daughter's Origami," "Green Line"
Wild Violet, "He Told Me It Would Happen"
Words & Images, "The Forest She Knows," "Three Short Poems"

"Autumn Lilies" won the 2011 Charlotte Miller Simon First Prize Poetry Award from the Ardmore, PA Free Library.

"Canoeing at Night" was runner-up in the 2011 *Philadelphia City Paper* Poetry Prize.

"The Mother as Persephone" also appears in *50 Women Over 50:A Celebration of Established and Emerging Writers* (PS Books, 2016).

"Wishbones" was reprinted in *Poetry Ink, 17ᵗʰ Annual* (Philadelphia, PA: Moonstone Arts Center, 2013)

"Spool" was reprinted in *Poetry Ink 18ᵗʰ Annual* (Philadelphia, PA: Moonstone Arts Center, 2014.)

www.ingramcontent.com/pod-product-compliance
Lightning Source LLC
Chambersburg PA
CBHW081135090426
42737CB00018B/3349